BROADWAY PLAY PUBLISHING, INC.

MOLLIE BAILEY'S
TRAVELING FAMILY CIRCUS:
FEATURING SCENES
FROM THE LIFE OF
MOTHER JONES

by

Megan Terry and JoAnne Metcalf

249 WEST 29 STREET NEW YORK NY 10   3820

MOLLIE BAILEY's TRAVELING FAMILY CIRCUS:
FEATURING SCENES FROM THE LIFE OF MOTHER JONES

Copyright 1983 book and lyrics by Megan Terry.
Copyright 1983 music by JoAnne Metcalf.

All rights reserved. This work is fully protected under the copyright laws of the United States of America.

No part of this publication may be photocopied, reproduced, stored in a retrieval system, or transmitted, in any form or by any means, electronic, mechanical, recording or otherwise without the prior permission of the publisher. Additional copies of this edition are available from the publisher.

Written permission is required for live performance of any sort. This includes readings, cuttings, scenes and excerpts. For amateur and stock performance, please contact Broadway Play Publishing, Inc.

For all other rights please contact Elisabeth Marton, 96 Fifth Ave., NY, NY 10011.

First printing: August 1983

ISBN: 0-88145-010-3

Cover art by William Sloan, Three
Design by Marie Donovan.
Set in Baskerville by BakerSmith Type, NYC.
Printed and bound by BookCrafters, Inc., Chelsea MI.

Author's Note:

This play is a presentation of imagined and possible events in the lives of two women who were born in the last century. These women were vibrant, positive, creative, strong and successful. They didn't know each other, but I believe we can know more about ourselves by knowing them.

—Megan Terry

Staging Notes:

Through the use of transformation techniques (or doubling, etc.) this show may be performed by seven or eight people, or as many actors as are available. The musical can also be successfully presented without scenery, costumes or props. It may also be produced with the most imaginative & complete scenic spectacle. The music may be provided by piano & percussion or a total orchestra. It can be staged & will work in any available space from an open room, through arena to proscenium.

PRODUCTION HISTORY

1. Mark Taper Laboratory Theater - their "Plays in Process" series, Los Angeles, California.

2. California Institute of the Arts, California.

3. Santa Barbara, California.

4. Omaha Magic Theater Workshop - Omaha, Nebraska.

5. Staged Reading at St. Scholastica College, Duluth, Minnesota - a joint production of St. Scholastica & University of Minnesota, Duluth.

CAST

MOLLIE BAILEY	MOTHER JONES
HER MOTHER	POLICE
HER FATHER	JUDGE
GUS - her husband	SOLDIER
*EUGENE	BRIDE
*BIRDA	WOMAN TEXTILE WORKER
*MINNIE	JACK BUCK - a mine owner
*MATTIE	WOMAN dressed in red
*W. K.	SHERIFF
*DIXIE	CIRCUS ANIMALS (may be played by animals or actors)
*ADA	CLOWNS
*ALLIE	MINERS
*BRAD-SCOTT	WOMEN
CHILDREN	

* Their children may be played by young people or adults.

PROLOGUE

Music intro.

Two Celtic queens cross the Irish Sea on a raft. Other members of their tribe are unconscious and lashed to the raft.

This scene should be played suspended over audience in center ring, either on trapeze or a device to give height. Unseen people below can manipulate ropes of the trapeze or flying harness holding the women, or it may also be played stationary but aloft, with the two women held up by actors or stagehands dressed in black. The two have to fight to hold their equilibrium during the stormy crossing. Their voices are fierce and commanding, with extremely harsh "R's' in the accents, but also warmth and humor should come through.

Storm sounds throughout scene can be produced by wind chimes, rolled cymbal, thunder machine, synthesized wind, etc.

MOTHER JONES: Did you lash down the males?

MOLLIE: Yes, Mother.

MOTHER JONES: Be sure their mouths are cleared. Seaweed can stop their breathing.

MOLLIE: Cut five more loose yesterday.

MOTHER JONES: Don't cut any more loose without letting me see them. Sometimes I can bring them back.

MOLLIE: We'd've capsized if I didn't let go the weak and the dead. We have two suckling boys. The mothers have sewn the boys' feet to the sides of their own thighs so the babes can't wash overboard. O Mother, I've never faced such a pressured sea.

MOTHER JONES: The barbarians will stay where it's easy to steal. They won't be following where we're going—it's too hard to get there.

MOLLIE: Mother, I love you so. Let me stand against the storm and spell you. If you hold my hand I'll be able to feel the way to steer.

MOTHER JONES: I can't see it but I smell the land. Look there, the kelp. Look there, the small fish . . .

MOLLIE: The storm wants to throw us back.

MOTHER JONES: No, we'll make land with at least one male in good condition.

MOLLIE: Why didn't we stop at the last island? The white cliffs were a beacon in the night.

MOTHER JONES: There's a greener land for us.

MOLLIE: Mother, let me take a turn against the sharks. I have sharp fins for ribs now and a will to feed the sharks to each other. Hold me fast before you sleep, then I can stand watch for a generation.

MOTHER JONES: Meave, Maya, Mary, hold on to my hair. The sea is high and killing.

MOLLIE: Mother, am I steering in the right direction?

MOTHER JONES: Yes, I'll close my eyes for a while.

MOLLIE: Stay near, in case I get in trouble.

MOTHER JONES: *(Warmly)* If we're not in trouble we're not going in the right direction.

ACT ONE

Circus music, band. A collage of circus sound, old and not so old songs and patriotic tunes. The medley possibilities are: "Old Gray Mare," "There'll Be a Hot Time in the Old Town Tonight," "Dixie," "Battle Hymn of the Republic," "Camptown Races," "Yankee Doodle," "Red River Valley," "Working on the Railroad," "Union Maid," "Rings on Her Fingers and Bells on Her Toes."

MOLLIE enters leading the opening extravaganza of the show to "Diamonds from the Stars." She flashes her large diamonds as she drives her carriage around the ring. She wears an elegant long gown of blue and silver (it has many breakaway sections for fast costume changes).

Her black hair shines in the glittering kerosene lights. She beams and lovingly welcomes the crowd with her eyes and mouth, she recognizes people she met last year, and pantomimes their names, as music blares. She nods, and has special waves and winks for children and young people. She salutes the older members of the audience.

Her carriage may be pulled by two actors dressed all in white with spangles, moving as horses. MOLLIE drives her carriage to the band stand, stands up in her carriage and addresses the audience, music under.

MOLLIE: Ladies and Gentlemen, the MOLLIE BAILEY– MOTHER JONES FAMILY CIRCUS welcomes you to another down-home good time show. We aim to please the little children, and make them laugh and sigh and when you grownups see them happy, you'll want to come by and see us here bringing clean family fun and wholesome cheer. The Mollie Bailey Family's been bringing you our circus every year since 1858. I am herself, Mollie Arline Kirkland Bailey, born in Alabama in 1844. And you know by now almost everyone calls me Aunt Mollie.

Fanfare.

MOLLIE: *(Continuing)* Ladies and Gentlemen and my friends, our children—prepare yourselves to view the most stupendous panoply of color and equestrienne ability ever displayed on the green earth of Texas, ever shown on the galloping grains of Kansas, ever glittered in the gold fields of California—the darlings you will see tonight who will sparkle before your eyes as the dew before God's, are my children and my children's children. Take it away—the MOLLIE BAILEY–MOTHER JONES circus history of two mothers, mothering the miners and the countryside, working every night and every day for motherhood, and sisterhood and brotherhood and The Union of the Workers, and the Union of Heaven with this beautiful Earth—I don't want the whole planet—a little piece two by six is all I need when my work is done. Let the show BEGIN.

Circus parade.

Fanfare. Begin song intro.

MOLLIE: *(At the band stand)* And now ladies and gentlemen, I want to introduce you to my children.

As she calls their names, they jump out from under her skirt. A trap door may be in the band stand, so endless streams of people seem to keep coming out from under her skirt. A parallel to the million clowns getting out of a teeny tiny car in modern circus acts.

MOLLIE: *(Continuing)* ADA! DIXIE! MATTIE! EUGENE! The best tuba player East or West of the Red River Valley! MINNIE! And then we made W.K., named for my father, although he never did get to see him since he disowned me . . . claimed I and the War, we broke his heart . . . ALLIE! BIRDA! BRAD-SCOTT!

BAILEY FAMILY CIRCUS SONG:
"We'll Melt You Down in Diamonds from the Stars"

CHORUS: *(All)* Oh we are wholesome, we are square.
  We count our blessings
MOLLIE & GUS: *(Spoken)* Our blessings are our children!
ALL: We hope you like us
  We love you and we care
  We don't fuss, we never cuss
  We're wholesome and we're square!

MEN: We love you and we love us.
  We love our Mother Mollie.
WOMEN: We love our Father Gus.
  We love our Father Gus.
ALL: The circus is a party,
  So come and live with us . . .

MOLLIE: Pack all your troubles in an old kit bag
  Tell them all you're leaving
  (and even though they're grieving)
  that it won't be for long;

QUARTET: We'll patch you right up
  and send you home with a song
ALL: Home with a song . . .
  home with a song . . .

MOLLIE: The circus is a party
  so come on, live with us! *(Kisses GUS)*
  We'll give you new clothes
  and a big red nose
  We'll love you all night,
  Turn your nose to a rose,
  We'll dust you with glitter
  and spangle your eyes
  We'll shine you with blue . . .
  . . . shine you with blue . . .

CHILDREN: Like our Father's eyes.

GUS & MOLLIE: Come to us, Darlin's,
    We'll melt you down in diamonds from the stars.
    Darlin', come ride
    Darlin', come ride
    Forever in our circus carts . . .

CHILDREN, MOLLIE & GUS: Come to us, Darlin's
    We'll melt you down in diamonds from the stars.
    Darlin', come ride
    Darlin', come ride
    Forever in our circus carts . . .

MOLLIE: *(Spoken)* The MOLLIE BAILEY–MOTHER JONES FAMILY OF WOMEN'S ETERNAL CIRCUS! We're all-round good people . . .

GUS: *(Spoken)* Right as rain on the open plain . . .

MOLLIE: *(Spoken)* Americans!

MOLLIE: . . . Sweet and Sane
    We built a country on a dare
    . . . cause we don't scare . . .
    We don't give up!

GUS: Our blessings are our children
    That makes us millionaires!

CHORUS: This is the way Mother Mollie taught us to live!
    We party and play
    but when folks are in trouble
    We give our hearts away!

    Oh, we are wholesome, we are square
    We count our blessings
    Our blessings are our children!

    Come to us darlin's
    We'll melt you down in
    diamonds from the stars!
    Darlin' come ride
    Darlin' come ride
    Forever in our circus carts.

Family dance.

BLACKOUT

Spot on MOLLIE.

MOLLIE: *(Timechange: as a very young person)* My dearest Father, I will go to my tree house which I built with my Nurse's son, Alexander, and think about all of this.

She climbs up pole or a knotted circus rope.

FATHER: I forbid . . .

MOLLIE: *(A quick climb down pole or rope)* I have carefully folded my quilt patterns, and practiced my dancing. I am a grown lady, Father. I am going to be married.

She grabs GUS's *hand and they run off around the ring. As they run he grows older till she helps him into a wheel chair and pushes it back up onto band stand.* MOLLIE *pushes* GUS *in wheel chair off the band stand and around the ring.*

MOLLIE: *(To audience)* Would you believe I ran away from home at fourteen to marry this gentleman?

GUS *leaps up and grows younger. One actor jumps on another's shoulders to play* MOLLIE's *father. Two women do the same to play* MOLLIE's *mother.* GUS *pantomimes playing violin. We hear the sound from the band stand.*

MOLLIE: *(In melodrama style)* O, my Angel Mother. O, my darling Mother. I've fallen wildly, passionately in love. It is just as you said it would be. He has swept me off my feet.

FATHER: That cheap musician is beneath you.

MOLLIE: But we love each other. We really love each other. He's asked me to marry him.

MOTHER: How wonderful. I approve of you, my beautiful child. You are in love. I love being in love. Tell me how you *knew* you loved him.

MOLLIE: He was standing in lantern light playing his violin. *(Violin music)* His own mother had introduced him, and the light was turning his red-blond hair into the Loving-light of Angels that always fly around the Holy Mother to love and protect her. And my heart began to shake, Mother. This light was lighting the head of my beloved. And his eyes were closed as he played. And the sight of his hair and the sweet lightness of his fiddle made my own heart burst open and fly to his head and enclose him.—At that moment—at that very moment, he opened his eyes, still playing such sweet sound on his violin. When I saw the light in his eyes, I left my seat and walked toward him. I was in a trance of divine love, Mother, of such energy and purity the likes of which I have never known. The entire audience seemed to feel as I did—there was a hush*(violin stops)*—an awesome hush—and then the applause didn't quit. I was at his feet by this time, and as he bowed to the applause, I told him, "I loved your music with all my heart and soul."

She has been walking to GUS *as she has been saying this while he plays in as spot. He bows, puts away his violin, takes her hand and kisses it.*

GUS: Will you walk with me to feel the moonlight?

Adoringly, she nods.

GUS: *(As they walk in a fallow spot)* Look at the horse tracks here. Want to follow them?

MOLLIE: We don't know where they go.

GUS: That's right.

MOLLIE: If you'll hold my hand, I won't be frightened.

GUS: What's your name?

MOLLIE: Mollie.

GUS: Mollie, you like music?

MOLLIE: I love *your* music.

GUS: *(Tripping)* WhoooooHa.

MOLLIE: *(Catches him)* I've got you.

GUS: *I* was supposed to take care of *you.*

MOLLIE: *(Holding him)* You're strong.

GUS: *(Feeling her)* So are you. How'd you get so strong?

MOLLIE: Playing piano, playing organ, building treehouses—

GUS: These horse tracks are leading us right up into the moonlight, and it seems to begin, the moonlight, does at the corners of your mouth—they're always smiling, even if you're not. You're the prettiest, strongest girl I ever met. *(Kisses her chin)*

MOLLIE: Sir! You kissed my chin.

GUS: I'm gonna do it again, I can't stop.

MOLLIE: But we're not married, it might be a sin?

GUS: Tastes so good, I can't stop, so you'll have to marry me. I'll have to marry you, and everyone will be happy. Would you be happy to have me kissing you like this, and this . . . all night and all day. We won't have to stop if we're married.

MOLLIE: But how would you have the time to play your violin?

GUS: That's why I love you so. You feel as warm and strong and cosy and vibrant as my fiddle. But you can kiss me back. Do it agin, oh kiss me, kiss me again.

MOLLIE: I can't.

GUS: Why not?

MOLLIE: I can't breathe. I can't get my breath.

GUS: Kiss me and let it go into my mouth.

MOLLIE: *(Shocked)* What? But sir!

GUS: Gus. Call me Gus. Your breath will come again. It's love
you're in. And that's passion took your breath away. Sink into
my arms. There, I've got you. Let it win. Ah, there, there,
there, see how good we feel? Hold me hard, again, Again.
Oh, my God, I've prayed to meet you. At last, a woman strong
as me! *(He pulls her down, and puts his head against her breast)*
Rock me. Hold me like you're never gonna see me again.

MOLLIE: I won't. You're leaving town with your family tonight.

GUS: That's right. Dear Mollie, if we get married, you'll come
too.

MOLLIE: My folks?

GUS: We'll run away.

MOLLIE: Your folks?

GUS: If you can hold me like this, we can be each other's folks.

MOLLIE: Sir, what am I doing to you that you love so much?

GUS: Through your touch I can feel the deep warm woman
strength that comes from your bones to mine. Our hearts are
keeping perfect time.

GUS: *(Sings "Hold Me and Rock Me")*
    Oh Hold me and rock me again, Mollie
    Hold me and rock me again
    Hold me and rock me again, Mollie
    I'll win the world for you, Mollie
    And I'll win it all over again
    Hold me and rock me, Mollie
    Oh, I'll win, I'll win, I'll win
    If you'll just hold me and rock me
    Hold me and rock me
    Oh, Mollie, just hold me and rock me again.

MOLLIE: I'll never leave you Gus. You don't have to win the world for me. Let's start our own circus and let the world own us.

MOLLIE & GUS: *(Duet)* Oh, Gus, Oh, Mollie
    Let's rock and hold us.
    Yes, Mollie, Gus, let the world
    Rock and hold us. *(Repeat)*

Re-enter scene with FATHER *and* MOTHER *clown and play as before. Music.*

FATHER: You're not marrying anyone, you're too young. You are confined to your room. I had forbidden you to go to that cheap circus show in the first place. If you'd obeyed your father, you wouldn't be that rat's slave now!

MOLLIE: Oh my Father, I disobeyed you and for that I am sorry, and I pray your forgiveness, but I'm thankful to the good Lord that I met and have fallen in love, in God's Love with Gus Bailey.

FATHER: Gus who? . . . You are not getting married!

MOLLIE *and* GUS *run off, circus music up. Circus clowns unfold and mime a fast parody of the scene.*

BLACKOUT

MOLLIE: And now ladies and gentlemen, a feat never before attempted by any circus from Roman times to the present. For the spiritual enlightenment and moral uplift of the peoples of Texas, Oklahoma, Alabama, Tennessee, Kansas, Nebraska, Arizona, New Mexico and the Territory of California—we will attempt with all care and humility to stage before your neighborly and attentive eyes—sections and scenes of sorrow and bravery, of secrecy and daring, scenes never before seen outside the deep of the woods, the bottom of an abandoned coal mine, the middle of an icy stream or upon the highways at midnight—This act has never been staged in America or on the continent, and it is offered to you tonight for the first time anywhere—ladies and gentlemen, I give you the one and only "Angel of the Miners," the little woman who walked miles on her own two feet to expose and put a stop to the vicious exploitation of children and adults and bring about the eight hour day—ladies and gentlemen, I give you a MOTHER— MOTHER JONES.

The lights go out. We dimly perceive candles and sighing off in the distance. Wheels are rolling against cobblestones. Slowly four small coffins come into view. Bodies of three girls and one boy lay nude on the top of the coffins. The coffins move in slow motion, pulled on two wheeled carts by old women. There is a candle on each corner of each coffin. MOTHER JONES *walks slowly, but not in the extreme slow motion of women pulling the coffins. She moves from body to body.*

MOTHER JONES: *(As she finishes washing each little body, she puts a white dress on it. Kisses it, holds it one more time, and then moves onto the next body.)* Goodbye , my darlings. We'll meet again. So many of us have died . . . there are crosses and crosses. Your grandmothers and your grandfathers whom you didn't get to see on this earth fought for generations to free Ireland. And your own dear father, who now lies near death himself from this terrible fever goes out fighting too. I am an American. My father brought me up that way too. I'm proud of America. I'm proud to be a citizen of this proud country. Here we have a chance to win in the struggle. So many have gone to their deaths with joy in their hearts to give us the chance to stand up and speak our minds. We owe these dead our gratitude, and we owe them our future acts. A strong and proud family, these fighters for freedom.

Exit cart.

MOTHER JONES *turns to address the audience—one candle lights her face—all other lights out.*

MOTHER JONES: In 1867, a yellow fever epidemic swept Mem-

phis. My husband was an iron moulder and a staunch member
of the Iron Moulders Union. The victims of yellow fever were
mainly among the poor and the workers. The rich fled the
city. People were not allowed to enter the house of a yellow
fever victim without permits. The dead surrounded us. They
were buried at night quickly and without ceremony. All about
my house I could hear weeping and the cries of delirium.
One by one, my four little children sickened and died. My
husband died. I sat alone through nights of grief. No one
came to me. No one could. Other homes were as stricken as
was mine. All day long, all night long, I heard the grating of
the wheels of the death cart.

There is a beat.

MOTHER JONES: I'll pray for my dead, but I make a covenant
with you Holy Mother Mary—I will find a way to fight for
the living. *(Sings "Fight Like Hell for the Living")*
    Hail Mary full of grace
    Never again will I
    see my child's living face.
    Holy Mary, Mother of God
    Mother my children
    Beside you in heaven.

    Take them to your bosom now
    And I vow
    To turn my heart
    to Mother those
    Still here in this vail of
    Tears and pain
    That their lives and their work
    Shall not be in vain.

    I will not turn my heart from you
    But I pledge to go on loving
    To extend my mothering
    To all the children
    Who work in the pits of the rich

To raise them up
To their rightful share
Of the fruits of your garden.

I will never stop loving our children
And I will take the strength you've given
Me in my rebirth
And extend the domain
Of your loving heaven
To cancel out the pain
In your living children
Here on earth.

Never let it be said, that I've
Turned my back on the dead.
I pray for them to live eternally
But I pledge all earthly gains
And my will
All my strength
All my days
And all my brains
To fight like hell for the LIVING!

Music, bright lights. MOTHER JONES *is gone. The canaries parade
around the ring. These can be actors with some plumage, or the actors
can create the bird characters through transformation and pantomime.*

MOLLIE: Ladies and gentlemen: my daughter, Birda, and her
fabulous fantastic fulcrum of fine feathered friends—at
great patience, care and with no tender concern withheld,
she has given these canaries that care that one would give
human beings who were preparing themselves for a career in
the great grand operas of Europe and New York and San
Francisco. Observe their deportment, and their ability to walk
while wearing gowns and ladies shoes, to say nothing of corsets.
Birda has trained her birds the way Gus and I have brought
up our children. The first song they've learned to sing in
public is:

BIRDA *conducts the canaries in the first verse of "Twinkle Twinkle Little Star." The canaries copy.*

BIRDS & BIRDA: Twinkle twinkle little star
  How I wonder what you are
  Up above the world so high
  Like a diamond in the sky.

MOLLIE: That's why I put all my spare change into diamonds, and I taught my children how to navigate from learning the stars.

Music.

MOLLIE *strides from the bandstand out into the ring, and takes up a buggy whip, and the rest fall into the buggy by her side or behind her as her children—the little circus box-like platforms can be arranged by the actors into a buggy or wagon as they regroup, or it can be pre-set this way.*

MOLLIE: *(Continuing)* I want you children to be comfortable on this earth, and the best way is to teach you that if you can see the stars, you'll never be lost. You can always judge your position and know your way home or to the next town where we have to play, if you can name the pictures the stars make up there. Now, Eugene, the sky is bright and sparkly and clear, what's the name of that set of stars right up there?

EUGENE: Big Dipper, Mama.

MOLLIE: *(Kissing him)* Right, my son. And Mattie, how do we know which way is North?

MATTIE: Uuuuhhhhhhhhhh.

BIRDA: Oh Mama, let me answer, I know the answer, I know it.

MOLLIE: Then tell it.

BIRDA: The pointer in the Big Dipper points toward the North Star. The tip of the tail of the Little Bear or the end of the handle of the Little Dipper.

MOLLIE: *(Hugging her)* Just like you, Birda, my Bright. I'm glad to see I didn't raise any dummies.

All the children laugh.

MOLLIE: The Dippers or the Bears are real close to us, so we can always feel at home. What's that way yonder?

ALLIE: The Milky Way.

MOLLIE: *(Sings, as does each one in the rest of this scene, "The Milky Way")*
    An Island Universe—the Milky Way—
    Someday we'll play there.
    There's another planet just like ours there,
    Some people say;
    And somewhere in that luminous tract
    We each have a twin
    A person who looks like us—exact!

ALL: Truth Mama?

EUGENE: A fact?

MOLLIE: Can't prove it, it's just what "some" people say,
    But I love to think about it—While we drive on our way—
    Thinking and singing right here
    We could still be singing to our twins up there.

MATTIE: Hello, Mattie Million Moons
    Beside the Little Bear . . .

EUGENE: Mattie, you're a loonie Luna.

ADA: Hello Ada Andromada—are you flipping there
    While I'm flipping here?

EUGEN: Ada, you make my stomach ache-a!

BIRDA: Birda shines on Orion's Star Belt.

EUGENE: Birda makes my Pegasus' heart melt-a!
    Eugene-nah, Pisces Neptun-ah!

ADA & MATTIE: Better known as the Little Dripper—Hey!

ALLIE: Eugene-nah—you can't be both a horse and a fish
    On the same day.

EUGENE: If a horse can have wings
    It can also have fins
    What do you say up there—my twins?

GUS: Yo ho Augustus Aquarius!

MOLLIE: Gus, Halley's Comet, Bailey!

GUS: Mollie Milky Way!

ALL: There's another Bailey Family Circus
    Playing near a star up there

MEN: The Bailey Family Circus plays on Mars today

WOMEN: We send our love and prayers to you our twins
    So many miles away.

ALL: Our Bailey Family Circus
    Will play ALL the stars
    One day!
    Tonight, we'll pitch our tent
    Along the Milky Way—

Lights fade as they drive, singing.

Music.

Lights up on MOTHER JONES.

MOTHER JONES *scene: transformation of her arrests.* MOTHER JONES
as herself, while the other actors play clown police and clown judges.

POLICE: Stop in the name of the law.

MOTHER JONES: You don't work for the law, you work for the
high class crooks.

POLICE: You're arrested in the name of puddin' tame.

MOTHER JONES: Take your hands off me you bloody, withered balled lice.

POLICE: State your name.

MOTHER JONES: Agitator, aggravator, hell raiser.

POLICE: That's a name?

MOTHER JONES: It's the name your paid press gave me.

POLICE: Where were you going?

MOTHER JONES: You knew in advance. You paid Pinkerton spies. You creeping skunk nosed blacklisting bandits! You know my movements before I can take my head up off my handbag and set my shoes East or West.

POLICE: All right Grandma, state your name and address.

MOTHER JONES: Mother Mary Harris Jones.

POLICE: Where do you live?

MOTHER JONES: Wherever there's a fight.

POLICE: Where have you been?

MOTHER JONES: Before the time of Christ, I sailed from Anatolia with Celtic Amazons. We lashed ourselves to log rafts, and braved the Irish Sea. I saw the British troops, when I was a child of three, march through Cork Streets with the heads of my dear martyred uncles, dripping Irish blood down the stuck-up British bayonets.

POLICE: Handcuff this scolding defiant old woman.

MOTHER JONES: *(Looking at cuffs)* Why thank you darlin', does this mean we're engaged? I know you can't help it honey, if you had your way you'd be on our side of the picket lines. You will too, one day.

POLICE: The captain says it's Revolution. We have to put you down.

MOTHER JONES: Haul back your gatling guns, you bums.

POLICE: The judge wants to see you, Mother Jones. *(He drags her to* JUDGE.*)*

Music.

ALL: *(Singing)* "The judge wants to see you, Mother Jones."

JUDGE: *(Pops out of a circus box)* The defendant will rise and state her name.

MOTHER JONES: Not to you, you scab. I wouldn't tell you the time of day.

JUDGE: You will address me as Your Honor, or I'll hold you in contempt.

MOTHER JONES: I am in contempt of you, you scab of the Capitalist robbers.

JUDGE: Who are you?

MOTHER JONES: Richard Harris' daughter.
    Mary Harris' child.
    Always obedient, always mild.

JUDGE: The papers says your mouth runs wild.

MOTHER JONES: The papers say what they're paid to say.

BAILIFF: Your name and address?

MOTHER JONES: My father's father was hanged
    In the fight for Ireland's freedom.
    My dad came here, looking for
    Spirit's kingdom.
    After he sailed, the bulldogs tore down
    Our dear cottage stone by stone. Even the
    Chimney God Bless us, looking for Father's
    Body. They all had the same grin behind
    Their mouths as you do.
    I spit on you, you scab.

JUDGE: I'm a Federal judge.

MOTHER JONES: I'm the rightful judge here.

JUDGE: Don't you fear the law?

MOTHER JONES: I don't see anything to fear. Not when there's such a big leer on the front of your bloody Corporate Capitalist Face.

JUDGE: I cannot forbear to express my great surprise that a woman of the apparent intelligence of Mrs. Jones should permit herself to be used as an instrument by designing and reckless agitators . . . in accomplishing an object which is entirely unworthy of a good woman. It seems to me that it would have been better far for her to follow the lines and paths which the Allwise Being intended for her sex to pursue. There are many charities in life which are open to her in which she could contribute largely to mankind in distress, as well as avocations and pursuits that she could engage in of a lawful character that would be more in keeping with what we have been taught and what experience has shown to be the true sphere of womanhood.

MOTHER JONES: The scab speaks! Scabby speech! Look boy, we're both aged and I hope we'll be able to be good friends when we meet again in heaven, but here in this hell you help to make on earth you're without honor in my eyes and a putrid scab for all the world to see.

JUDGE: *(To audience)* I don't know whether to put her behind bars or salt her down in the looney bin. Let's see if sixty days will shut her up.

They drag her off and put her in a jail cell. The rats start to rush in at her feet. Rat sounds.

MOTHER JONES: Get back, get back. I like you better than the ones in the courtroom. Your sharp teeth are all out front. No masks and robes to hide behind.

POLICE GUARD: What do you do?

MOTHER JONES: I sew rather than boss little children. My tiny babes, spotted and yellow eyes, yellow Irish eyes. Then yellow bodies, then black spots on the yellow, and black vomit pouring from the mouths I kissed so much. And then their little black bodies eternally cold to my touch. I'll make war on your monopoly industries. Starvation wages you've paid out in nightmares to little children and their sacred Mothers. Class-assed Limey, Episcopalian, Christ kissing, money grubbing, life killing, spirit squashing Capitalist burglars. You've stolen the land, and you make them work their own ground and then they have to buy bread from the underpaying, lying, thieving, likes of thieving, stealing you. Go to hell, cause I'm gonna raise it all around you if you don't. *(Quietly, to the audience. Music underscore.)* I heard President Lincoln speak many times, and I sewed Mrs. Lincoln's Inaugural gown.

BLACKOUT

At night in the wagon, the children are asleep.

GUS *drives while* MOLLIE *plays on her portable organ. The horse is walking very slow.*

MOLLIE *keeps playing the opening bars of "The Old Gray Mare" as she speaks to* GUS.

MOLLIE: Mr. Bailey?

GUS: Yup, Mrs. Bailey . . .

MOLLIE: Mr. Bailey . . . I love our life . . .

GUS: Me too.

MOLLIE: Mr. Bailey, it's so perfect, except . . .

GUS: Except . . .

MOLLIE: Only thing keeps it from being God's perfect creation, here we are, we have our animals, our children, and . . .

GUS: And you've collected enough plants to make this wagon the "Rolling Garden of Eden."

She leans over and kisses him.

MOLLIE: I love the way you talk.

GUS: I love the way you play.

MOLLIE: I love the way you walk..

GUS: Did you think it'd last so long?

MOLLIE: God meant it too. If only father hadn't turned to stone.

GUS: He loves you much as me, and you know how he saw me!

MOLLIE: I guess I can't have everything. If I did, I couldn't see so clearly what I do have. *(She plays more bars of "Old Gray Mare.")* Do you still love me?

GUS: I'd say. We got enough children to prove that.

MOLLIE: *(Pressing her belly)* And another on the way. Mr. Bailey . . . the only thing that really pains me is that my father, a man of great strength and dignity . . .

GUS: *(Smiling)* Till he lost the war . . .

MOLLIE: He'll never recover . . .

GUS: Nope . . .

MOLLIE: Why can't he see the man in you? The gentle beautiful, dear, strong man I saw in you at fourteen, and I see it anew every time I look at you. Mr. Bailey?

GUS: Yes, Mrs. Bailey?

MOLLIE: I love you . . . I do . . . I keep hearing this music pattern all the time now, when we're travelling between the towns. It won't leave me alone. Could you think up some words for it to give it an anchor? Then my head will be cleared for something new.

GUS *hums with her playing for a minute and begins to sing words of "Old Gray Mare."*

MOLLIE *laughs in counter point and mouths to the audience on line* "*She ain't what she used to be," she pantomimes: "Oh, yes she is, and better!"*

They kiss.

BLACKOUT

MOTHER JONES *walks up to a teenage soldier. She has her handbag and a few newspapers under her arm.*

MOTHER JONES: Good day to you, son.

SOLDIER: How 'do M'am.

MOTHER JONES: And what are you guarding, son?

SOLDIER: Fort Omaha, M'am.

MOTHER JONES: Been in Omaha long?

SOLDIER: Six months, M'am.

MOTHER JONES: Friendly town?

SOLDIER: *(Nods)* Biggest town I ever seen.

MOTHER JONES: Just right I'd say—I come here to rest and visit now and then.

SOLDIER: You shouldn't walk too far unescorted, M'am—some people here gits out of hand, drinkin' and fightin'—time to time.

MOTHER JONES: Don't begrudge the working man his drink. It's the only vacation he can afford.

SOLDIER: M'am?

MOTHER JONES: Whiskey's a mighty small luxury compared to how many hours a fellow has to work for his boss. *(Pulls out a flask)* Have a shot?

SOLDIER: Why, thank you M'am.

MOTHER JONES: Comes from one of the finest stills in Homestead, Pennsylvania.

SOLDIER: *(Pulls on flask)* M'am, that's right smooth!

MOTHER JONES: Yes, it is that. Glad to see you're a discriminating fellow.

SOLDIER: Yes M'am.

MOTHER JONES: Where you from, son?

SOLDIER: Red Cloud, M'am.

MOTHER JONES: Pretty country down that way—passed through Red Cloud on my way to Colorado.

SOLDIER: Never been that far. Ah dream about the mountains.

MOTHER JONES: Colorado fishing is good, lad. I was wading an ice cold stream one day on my way up to a mining town near Trinidad, Colorado and when I got to the other bank, I found two fat rainbow trout caught in my petticoat. A good fourteen inches—the both of them.

SOLDIER: *(Laughing and blushing)* Ah never heard a fish story such as that, M'am.

MOTHER JONES: 'Tis the truth, lad. But you can't be much used to the truth with nothing to read here but the Omaha Morning Herald.

SOLDIER: I like to read M'am and I try to do it often as I can get the time. My Daddy can't read but he tanned my hide to make sure I would.

MOTHER JONES: I have a paper here'll help educate you, lad—"Appeal to Reason"—It's addressed to young men like you who need to know the truth and want to better themselves. What's your Daddy do for a living?

SOLDIER: Hired man, M'am—that's why I joined the militia. No way to get land myself far as I could see.

MOTHER JONES: Tell you what I'll do, son. I'm gonna give you a free subscription to "Appeal to Reason." You get the truth from this paper—the Omaha Morning Herald just prints the lies and handouts of the Robber Baron Railroad Land grabbers and the Capitalist Corporate Robbers. You help me sell more subscriptions among the barrack mates and I'll see you get 5¢ for yourself on every sale you make.

SOLDIER: Yes, M'am!

MOTHER JONES: You won't have any trouble selling, son—because you are getting out the word of truth—to every one of your friends. You soldiers are all the sons of working men and you got to have the facts of life close at hand if you're ever to get your proper share of the wealth of this great country. Shall we have another dram?

Lights fade.

Circus training ring: BIRDA, MOLLIE & BIRDA's *horse.*

BIRDA: Mother, I'm having such a good time today. I'm allowing myself to say everything that comes into my head. It's so much fun, it makes me feel like I'm flying.

MOLLIE: That's a nice vacation for you, my darling, but do learn which people to do that with.

BIRDA: With you, Mother, with you and my beautiful horse.

MOLLIE: Yes, my darling Birda, you train yourself right and then you'll have the power to train your animal. *(Kissing her on forehead)* This is the first animal you get to organize, then you can do it with fourfooted ones.

BIRDA, *alone with her horse, as the band plays "Shenandoah." She is trying to teach her horse to dance. The horse is played by one person. She will mount the horse by end of scene and go off stage and out of room at a flying gallop.*

BIRDA: I can walk, and you can walk. I can tie my shoelaces, and I know for certain that I can tell the time my dear, my beautiful beast. How I love my beast. I love you. I love your shining coat, and your eyes melt my heart. I was so embarrassed for so long beast, you know I only pretended to be able to tell the time. Yes, there's a beast, oh how beautiful you will be when you know all the steps, yes, there's my beast. Oh my beast you have a beautiful way of bowing on the beat. I want to fly with you. Just you learn to dance and then we will sneak away just you and I and we'll go out to the lush green bayous down by the river, and I'll bathe the sweat off your beautiful strong and perfect backside. Oh you do have a marvelous bottom my beast. I adore your magnificent and monarchly head but I have to tell you how I also adore your behind. Yes, there's a beast, that's my beast, my beast is beautiful, my beast is a beauty. Yes, raise your foot again my beauty, just ever so such a shade higher, yes, my beauty. I love you to do it that way. Yes, my beauty, you make me proud. My heart is flying, go back to the beginning my perfection and then, right, right, yes there's my beauty. How grand you will be in your harness, I'll make you the most shining and perfect, and you know between you and I, you are the true star of my circus. Yes, there's my—no, no, darling, go back, you've nearly got it, yes again, again, perfect. *(Hugs horse passionately, throws herself up on horse's back, throws down her training whip.)* Now we'll gallop all the way out to the cliffs above the river and we'll fly right off and up into the sky. We'll fly, we'll fly . . .

Circus music up.

END OF SCENE

END OF ACT ONE

ACT TWO

MOTHER JONES: *The circus tent is dark. From a distance we hear* MOTHER JONES' *voice singing as she walks to keep herself company. She carries a lantern to light her way, or she is lit by moonlight that follows her like a new moon follow spot. She gets closer and closer and comes into view as she sings. She walks across the stage and out and exits, still singing, and then reappears at another exit, walks cross the other side of the stage and disappears through another exit singing. Nothing else happens but night sounds, rushing water sounds, moonlight, or lantern light, and* MOTHER JONES *singing. The singing trails off in the distance on the exit—but it should have feeling of a continuous song rather than one with a "set" ending. She might also be dodging bullets from unseen guns as she goes.*

MOTHER JONES: *(Sings "I Was Born in Revolution")*
    I was born in revolution
    in revolution will I stay.
    (Spoken) Till I soften the hardened hearts
    of the Capitalist Corporations
    To the miners' right
    To an eight hour day.

    I was born in revolution
    Some eighty years ago,
    In the rainbow greens of Ireland's Dream *(Pause)*
    (Spoken) To throw the Murderers out . . .
    And set us again
    on the dancing path
    Where once we'd been
    Before the British slammed
    their military down the Irish throats.
    And darkened our song
    and spotted our pride
    and forced our Queens and Heros
    to hide down in the caves
    of our swollen hearts. *(Pause)*

And down the generations we hear
the grieving keen
Throw the thieves and robbers out
We've not given up our dream
For Freedom!

I was born in revolution
I've fought eighty years for you
and I've made a pact with God
To stay another eighty
till I see my boys—
have won the fight
to control their days
and love their nights . . .

Listen to me boys, Mother is with you . . .
And I'll never leave you,
Till we've seen these troubles through.

I was born to be with you in revolution.
I was born to serve you in revolution
I was born in revolution . . .
Listen to me boys . . .
Mother is with you . . .
. . . And I'll never leave you . . .
. . . Till we've seen these troubles through . . .

MOTHER JONES' *voice trails off as she hums or whistles.*

END SCENE

EUGENE, *the eldest son of* MOLLIE *and* GUS, *brings in the woman he wants to marry. Throughout this scene, other children and circus members can be seen rehearsing and therefore converging in main scene and then recede to other areas of focus according to director's discretion.*

EUGENE: Mother . . . Father . . . Mrs. Bailey . . . and   Mr. Bailey . . .   MY DEAR PARENTS . . . I want to present to you . . . a creature who has captured my heart and soul.

The woman shyly comes forward and bows to MOLLIE *and* GUS.

EUGENE: *(Continues)* We met after the last show. She fell in love with my reflection in the light of the sound of my coronet playing, just like you said it would be, Mother.

MOLLIE: Who said that?

GUS: You must have told him the story of how you fell in love with me.

MOLLIE: It takes two to Polka.

GUS: I'd rather Schottische.

MOLLIE: Hello, little lady, can you dance?

PROSPECTIVE BRIDE: I twirl, Madam.

MOLLIE: That's usually involved in most dances.

BRIDE: Your son is so handsome.

MOLLIE: He's a loving son.

BRIDE: He's a fine musician.

MOLLIE: He's growing all the time. That's the great thing about having children—seeing they grow up well. God let's us guard them for a little while . . .

GUS: Do you play or dance?

The BRIDE *displays whatever form of play, tricks, gifts the woman playing the part has within her, i.e., singing-tumbling-etc.*

GUS: *(Looking at* MOLLIE*)* She could work out very well.

MOLLIE: I like your skin. I see your eyes are clear and earnest. I love my son, and I want him to be as happy as I am with my husband, but there is one other thing we have to get to if you're to join our family—our work.

BRIDE: I love Eugene, I'll cook for him, I'll keep his clothes, I'll make him happy, I'll learn his favorite foods.

MOLLIE: *(Matter-of-fact)* It's a hard life, but it's clean. We care for ourselves and we love the folks who support us. We see the same folks every year and we give them a show that's more than they paid for.

EUGENE: Mother, I love her.

MOLLIE: *(Warmly)* Eugene! You're full of love. You were brought up that way. But not everyone has been so fortunate as to have me, your Mother Mollie, and my darling, your Father Gus, and our dear neighbors the audience as a constant teacher.

BRIDE: I'm pious, I pray to God. I pray for guidance. And I pray to our ancestors to help me carry on.

MOLLIE: I like the tone of your voice. I love the tilt of your smile, and I adore the color of your skin. It's sunny even when the clouds are out. But some folks would think this circus is a hard life, and I don't want to mislead you.

BRIDE: I'm a very good girl. I'm so in love with your son.

EUGENE: That's why we must be married.

GUSS: But you're so young.

MOLLIE: And so were we.

GUS: Fourteen was old in those days; most people died by twenty.

MOLLIE: We live longer now, and . . .

BIRDA: Mother, she loves him. She anchors and spines him. Eugene gets carried away and sometimes he could evaporate, . . . no one can play coronet like him. Oh, please, do let them get married, and we'll have one more instead of one less.

GUS: She's so lovely, and she'll make lovely children like you did.

MOLLIE: Flattery will get you everywhere . . . witness . . . nine children!

All the other children come forward and improvise a small trick, stunt, or tiny improvisation with the bride as the others speak. The animals too come to sniff her out.

EUGENE: Mother, you ran away when you were a child so you could marry father.

MOLLIE: I was born when I was already ten thousand years old.

EUGENE: I give up!

MOLLIE: I adore you.

EUGENE: I love you too, mother, and I want you to love the woman I love.

MOLLIE: I want to, but there's a lot at stake.

EUGENE: I thought love was all.

MOLLIE: That's a saying. A good sweet taste, a fine illusion, but living on the road, day after day without diminishing one's soul, are you sure she's what you want. She could be a profound intrusion.

EUGENE: She'll expand me! She has a beautiful soul, so clean, so pure, so white.

MOLLIE: *(To audience and all)* Right away I'm alarmed!

EUGENE: But those are all perfect qualities.

GUS: To a tent preacher, but not to us!

MOLLIE: Your father is right.

EUGENE: She has a clean soul.

MOLLIE: Then don't marry her.

EUGENE: I don't understand you.

MOLLIE: You can marry her if her soul is as patched as our tent.

EUGENE: Mother, why are you trying to hurt me when I'm most in love?

MOLLIE: Because I *do* love *you.*

GUS: First born, love child. We love you. We want you to have the love we've had.

EUGENE: Do you have to say all this in front of her?

MOLLIE: It's in front of *you*, and since when have we not been a family.

GUS: Look, son, if we have to watch what we say, we can't be who we are. And if you don't want to be who we are; then, you'll have to think about going away.

EUGENE: But this is my life and I want her for my wife. She has a pure soul.

MOLLIE: Is that the way you think about yourself, too?

EUGENE: *(A tiny bit smug)* I certainly hope so.

MOLLIE *looking at* GUS *and shrugging. They kiss, and holding hands, do a motion polka as the following speech occurs led by* MOLLIE. GUS *comes in on certain lines, chosen by you, the director, at crucial points, on a different musical note, so that it gives the effect of minor-key harmony without any written music.*

MOLLIE, *the lead speaker, with* GUS, *and sometimes the children coming in exactly or a little bit late on certain lines, to make speaking music.*

MOLLIE: My son, and all my children. You know the reason we have a good life, and fine audiences and our business increases year by year is because we don't skimp on love. We pull out all the stops for spirit. We enhance our private dramas, sing our pain, and we catapult our pleasure from cannons. Gunpowder is reversed, but at the same time we do not kid ourselves that there is only one dimension to this place. And our entire contract with God is working toward that state of promised grace. Please Eugene! I love you, but don't forget, I'm your mother and I know you. You think I love only the good in you? You think to sell us your bride, by showing only her pure points. That's not what circus is all about. Where are the falls? Falling and almost falling and recovering from falling. That's our job.

EUGENE: She's good.

MOLLIE: Stop harping on that. Find out the worst. Most people are so short-sighted they assume that their "good" soul, if it is really a soul and a transmitter between this world and the next, cannot be only someone's, anyone's, my one's, your one's, idea of what is good; it must also embody bad, bumbling, belligerance, balderdash bereavement, beauty, black and bruised as well as the sunny side of the street. If the soul is a soul that is whole, it must be made up of all aspects, dark and light, of the human/animal possibilities.

EUGENE: *(Frightened and almost exasperated)* Mother . . . you ask for everything!

MOLLIE: You bet your bottom boots and why NOT?????

A moment as they look at each other.

EUGENE: Mother and Father, I see she's too good for us. And I'm going to marry her, no matter what you say.

MOLLIE *and* GUS *smile and kiss each other and then* EUGENE *and his* BRIDE *to be, much to their bewilderment.* MOLLIE *and* GUS *sing together and do a soft shoe to a shortened verions of "I Had a Dream Dear."*

MOLLIE & GUS: *(To the tune of "I Had a Dream Dear")*
    In that case, we give—
    Our consent to you—
    We had that dream dear,
    Our son, it was of you.
    Come here, our darlings, dance to—
    Bailey's circus time.
    Fun is our dream dear
    Will you give it time . . .

MOLLIE *at the end of the dance addresses audience.*

MOLLIE: My friends, I know it is necessary that we all pray for, and love, as well as, respect the dead, but please, don't forget to *play* with the *young*.

BLACKOUT

MOTHER JONES *and three children are walking down the railroad tracks.*

CHILD: There's our house, up there, Mother Jones.

MOTHER JONES: You're sure you have room for me?

BOY: We only got one bed.

GIRL: But there's enough room for you.

CHILD: You'll keep us warm.

MOTHER JONES: Ah, the floor will do fine. My handbag will be my pillow.

CHILD: I want to carry it. It's so round.

MOTHER JONES: The world is round, the stars are round, and you have the darling round face of a dear cherub.

CHILD: *(Running around* MOTHER JONES*)* I'm round.

BOY: I'm tall.

GIRL: I'm taller.

CHILD: We're round—Mother's round.

GIRL & BOY: You're short.

CHILD: I'm round. I'm round.

GIRL & BOY: Prove it.

CHILD: I can run around you.

GIRL: You're not gonna give me the run around, 'cause I'll jump over you. *(She does)* There—you're short!

CHILD: *(To* BOY) You're round.

BOY: *(Jumping over her)* You're short.

CHILD: Short don't keep me from being round.

CHILD *runs around her sister and brother singing "We're round, we're round, we're all round."* MOTHER JONES *takes up the song too, and finally the* GIRL *and* BOY *join in and laugh.*

MOTHER JONES *and the three children enter the hovel. Their* MOTHER *has a new baby in her arms.*

MOTHER JONES: How old is the baby?

WOMAN: Three days. Went back to the mill this morning. The Boss was good and saved my place.

MOTHER JONES: When did you leave?

WOMAN: The boss was good, he let me off early the night the baby was born.

MOTHER JONES: Where's your husband?

WOMAN: My darling, bless his soul, is in heaven these five months now.

MOTHER JONES: What do you do with the baby while you work?

WOMAN: Oh, the boss is good and he lets me have a little box with a pillow in it beside the loom. The baby sleeps there and when he cries, I nurse it.

MOTHER JONES: *(Reaching for baby and holding it)* Ah darlin' so you've listened to the whiz and whir of machinery before you came into the world, and now you're here, your dear ears hear nothing but the incessant racket of the machines raining down on this wee skull like iron rain—and you'll be a wage earner, too, a man at six years, bringing ten cents a day home to Mama? *(To the* MOTHER) How much do you earn?

WOMAN: *(Looking down)* Mother, after food and rent is taken out, our wages leaves nothing left over from a whole year's work.

MOTHER JONES: I'm going to get you out of here to a town where you can start over.

WOMAN: But we can't leave. We're in debt.

MOTHER JONES: Do you want to see your babies die here in front of your eyes?

WOMAN: No, Mother, no.

MOTHER JONES: I'll take you to another state! You can start again—free and clear—a fighting chance at last . . .

WOMAN: Oh, Mother, I'm afraid.

BOY: They'll shoot us if we try to run away.

MOTHER JONES: We're catching the midnight train.

WOMAN: But I have no cash.

MOTHER JONES: Neither do I. *(Conspiring and laughing, and giving back the baby and hugging them all)* But the railroad men are friends of mine, they'll take us to another city; we'll invent you a new name and get you a fresh start. That's how we settle debts with slave masters. Hurry darlins'; let's bundle up your things. When it's pitch black, we'll sneak down to the tracks and wait for our friends . . .

As lights fade down, sound of train approaching in distance.

A circus tent, lights up on rehearsal trapeze.

The others are working out—setting up their acts, etc. MINNIE *keeps falling or losing her grip on the trapeze or missing her flips.* BIRDA *gives her a searching look.*

MINNIE: Birda, Birda, am I love sick or do I have Spring fever?

BIRDA: Six of one, half dozen of the other.

MINNIE: Can't work, I'm off in a dream. This morning I fell off the trapeze. *(She rubs her head)*

BIRDA: *(Feeling* MINNIE's *head)* That's an ostrich egg. Who's the bird dog?

MINNIE: Then it's love?

BIRDA: You better do something about it before you crack your skull.

MINNIE: But he wants me to quit the circus.

BIRDA: What can *he* do?

MINNIE: He catches more catfish than anyone else in his county.

BIRDA: What else?

MINNIE: He makes me dizzy.

BIRDA: The fall made you dizzy.

MINNIE: No, I was thinking of him. I see his body walking everywhere.

BIRDA: Toward you or away?

MINNIE: That's what frightens me. Every time I think about him, I see him walking away from me—and—*(She demonstrates)*

MINNIE: *(Singing)* He has such a manly walk,
    And one of the foremost
    Of his many charms
    Is the way blond hair grows
    On his thick strong arms;
    A dimple flashes here near his chin
    When he locks my eyes and grins
    His mind melting grin;
    His beauty is such a glorious shock
    I want to cleave to him now
    As my only rock;
    But what really causes my loving heart to knock
    Is the way his broad shoulders sway
    When my manly man walks
    His manly walk.

BIRDA: Hmmmmmmm. Yes, that's a walk all right.

MINNIE: I'm so love sick, I can't move. Can't play my horn, I don't want to eat. I can't think.

BIRDA: And you can't talk

They laugh together.

MINNIE: Do you think mother and dad would be upset if I quit?

BIRDA: Why can't *he* join *us?*

MINNIE: He feels sorry for us.

BIRDA: That settles it.

MINNIE: I should marry him?

BIRDA: Forget him.

MINNIE: But I'm lovesick!

BIRDA: Sounds painful. Go back to work.

MINNIE: I should have expected you to act this way. You have a young man in every other town. I fear you'll never settle down and be faithful.

BIRDA: Settle down! I see myself more settled than any of you, except mother. Settle down! I love work. I love our animals and I *am* faithful, I have the greatest feeling of fidelity to our audiences. I've never had an accident in public. Knock on wood! *(She knocks on her own head at this saying)* The people know us. They're our friends and they trust us to lift up their spirits. Once a year they can get out of the mud and see some color, some light wholesome fun and fine music, and some mighty excellent performing. We're getting better every year.

MINNIE: You equate love of your work with love of a man?

BIRDA: What could be the difference?

MINNIE: We're created in God's image.

BIRDA: When man gets as much sense as animals, I'll take another look at him.

MINNIE: Birda, you don't like anything unless it has fur or feathers.

BIRDA: You're right. *(Sings "His Horsey Walk")*
　　He has such a majestic walk;
　　And one of the foremost of his many charms
　　Is the way white hair grows
　　On his thick forelock
　　A dimple flashes here near his nose
　　When he locks my eyes and snorts
　　I vault to his back leaping only from my toes
　　His beauty is such a glorious shock
　　I love him from his big brown eyes
　　To his *four* white socks;
　　But what really causes my loving heart to knock
　　Is the way his broad rump sways
　　When my majestic horse walks
　　His horsey walk.

MINNIE: I love you, sister.

BIRDA: *(Embracing her)* I don't want to be binding up broken bones from your love sick falls . . . have babies, and send them back to me to train. *(She laughs and pets* MINNIE'*s face)* You are growing up. Your beautiful skull is beginning to show. These cheekbones are especially fine . . .

MINNIE: Do you think you'll ever fall in love?

BIRDA: You little monkey! I've been in love ever since I was placed alive on mother's breast. Who else has trained canaries to sing like Metropolitan Opera stars? Who else has . . . taught a wild horse to dance like Pavlova . . . who else . . . *(Her voice fades as they walk into next scene)*

Reprise: "His Manly Walk/His Horsey Walk"

A man confronts MOTHER JONES *as she leads a parade of striking Mine Workers' children.*

MINE OWNER: Now Mary . . . why don't you come home with me for a spot of good brandy and . . .

MOTHER JONES: Mrs. Jones to you, you low down, no good . . .

MINE OWNER: Mrs. Mother Mary Jones—you've known me more'n ten years now. I was a grubbing miner too . . .

MOTHER JONES: You're a working man no more, Jack Buck— You're an Empire!

MINE OWNER: I built all the mines in this hollow with my own two hands.

MOTHER JONES: If you did that with those hands alone, you'd be B.S.ing with God by now and not with me. You've stolen this land and I watched you do it.

MINE OWNER: You know, you're the only woman I ever cared a snap about—I still want to marry you—We've been as close as bugs in a rug in the past.

MOTHER JONES: Past is past. I look at you now and I see "Boss"—"King"—"Boss"! You've crossed over the line and stolen from your own class, you low down dirty son-of-a-bitch, we'll whip you yet! We're winning this strike.

MINE OWNER: But, Mary, how can you treat me like this when you've shared my bed?

MOTHER JONES: That's a wishful, dirty, willful lie!

MINE OWNER: I'll tell the miners how you slept with me and cried my name thirteen times before the dawn. Mary, you made me so proud I marked the tally on the wall. You're a mighty woman, Mary Harris Jones and I want you back in my bed.

MOTHER JONES: Mule Shit means more to me than you do— You turncoat robber bastard of British spawn!

MINE OWNER: I'm as Irish as you, Mary Harris.

MOTHER JONES: That's another lie. I see nothing but British Buckingham written all over your two faces.

MINE OWNER: Mary, dear, Ah I love the flash in your eyes—go away now and leave my men alone. You know me, you know my company will take care of them.

MOTHER JONES: Leave them under the care of your company, hey? *(She singles out a young girl)* What do you have there in your little package, my darlin'?

GIRL: *(shyly)* Apples from the company store, Mother.

MOTHER JONES: *(Opening bag and then with fire in her eyes, she tells MINE OWNER)* See! *(Shows to all around)* Here is a pound of dried apples. Rotten. Look at these rotten apples crawling with worms. Worms! You make your workers sweat 14 hours a day and you have the gall to sell them worms. Death alone will make me give the care of these poor souls to you. For shame Jack Buck. You're a thief and a traitor. A traitor to your own class.

MINE OWNER: You won't be here long, there's a $1000 price on your head.

MOTHER JONES: That's another lie you stingy bastard. The price on my head is $5,000.

BLACKOUT

Spotlight up on MOLLIE. *She addresses the audience.*

MOLLIE: Ladies and Gentlemen: We will show you how to work. Some people have put forward the notion that women don't know how to organize, don't know how to make decisions, don't understand logic, nor can they even tell a story with a beginning and a middle and an end. I confess, to the last accusation, because the way I see it the story has no beginning and it not only hasn't ended for me, it's always starting all over again. In fact, ladies, gentlemen aren't interested in this sort of knowledge. What I want to tell the ladies is, that the way to stay young, to have eternal life and long eyelashes and beautiful skin, is not to paste yourselves up with creams and poltices, but to start over. Take a risk on yourself; Mother Mary Harris Jones is one first class risk taker—that's why I want our dear friends—our audience, to experience her. She has a different way of living in this world than do I and a different philosophy of life—she gave away her money as she made it while I bought a bit of land in each and every town we ever played. I wanted to make sure no one could keep me from playing if I wanted to. They can't run you off your own land. Sometimes to minimize danger you have to take risks, change your address, let it all go, move on—the essence of staying young is to start all over again. That goes for heavenly and human bodies. I think we can all agree—IT'S ABOUT TIME!

LIGHTS DIM

TIME SHIFT

One of the first phones rings in the dark.

MOTHER JONES: Hello!

HAGGERTY: *(On line)* Oh, Mother, come over quick and help us. The boys are that despondent. They're going back Monday . . .

MOTHER JONES: I'll be there. I'm holding a meeting here tonight, but I'll leave at daybreak.

Lights come up. MOTHER JONES *walking into light carrying a lantern.*

MAN: *(Rigid with fright)* You Mother Jones?

MOTHER JONES: Yes, I'm Mother Jones.

MAN: The superintendent told me that if you came down here he would blow out your brains. He said he didn't want to see you 'round these parts.

MOTHER JONES: Tell that superintendent—I'm not come to see him. I'm coming to see the miners.

ANOTHER MAN: *(Runs up to* MOTHER JONES—*he is skin and bones)* Do you see these cars over there, Mother? *(Pointing)* On the siding? We made a contract with the coal company to fill those cars for so much, and after we had made the contract, they put lower bottoms in the cars, so they'd hold yet another ton. I've worked for this company all my life and all I have now is this worn-out frame.

MOTHER JONES: Lead me to the hall, I'm holding a meeting.

MAN: Won't let us use the hall. Company owns it.

MOTHER JONES: The church?

ANOTHER MAN: They own the ground it's built on and said they'd take it back.

MOTHER JONES: Spread the word! We'll meet at the four corners of the public road.

Men dash off.

MOTHER JONES *gets up on box and addresses the audience as if they were the miners. Actors straggle in like those late to a meeting as* MOTHER JONES *speaks.*

MOTHER JONES: Boys, I know how hard it's been. This strike has been goin' on five months now, and you've stood your ground and shown you're men. More than seven thousand of your brothers have died in the mines here in the last twenty years, and what have you got to show for it? There's no law to protect your life nor limb, and none to protect your job. You know coal company recruiters are in Europe at this very minute living in palace hotels, and drinking 50 year old brandy while they solicit more cheap immigrant labor. Bill Phipps, you're working fourteen hours a day now and can't get ahead. The company owns everything, but this public corner we're standing on. Where I come from we wouldn't ask the pigs to live in the shacks the company gives you. The United Mine Workers has decided to work with you for human conditions for human beings. Are you company dogs boys, or are you human beings?

Crowd responds.

MOTHER JONES: Then don't go back to work, boys. The Negro slave possessed advantages that the white laboring man has not. When the slave was ill his master cured him; the company makes you dig two tons of coal to pay the company doctor; when the slave was hungry he was fed; the company charges you nine tons of coal to eat; when the slave was naked he was clothed. Nobody is doing this for you. You pity yourselves but don't pity your brothers, or you would stand together to help one another. You've got to take the pledge. Rise and pledge to stick to your brothers and the Union till the strike's won!

Men shuffle their feet and stay seated. Women rise, some with babies in their arms, others with children hanging onto their skirts.

WOMEN: *(Divide the lines among the actors)*
I pledge, Mother!
We're with you, Mother!
No one from our house is goin' to work tomorrow, Mother!
The strike is still on!
We're not slaves, Mother!
My man ain't goin'!
I give you my solemn pledge, to see no one goes to work in that mine!

WOMAN ONE: Listen to me, neighbors. We kept Mother Jones all night in our house, and you know—all of you know what the coal company did. They sent the Sheriff at the crack of dawn to throw this Angel, sent to us by God, out into the road. And then the company directed the Sheriff to evict my family and me from that miserable shack they called our home. In this small wagon is what was in our house; a picture of the Blessed Virgin, a picture of her son, Jesus, a few pots and dishes, a bedstead, a table and two chairs. Our earthly possessions from working fifteen years for fat masters. Because we were good Samaritans last night, shared our roof with this dear woman, the company has thrown us out, robbed us of bed and shelter. They're afraid of a grandmother!—and you men are afraid of the company? We're on the edge of the world now—There's no more room to be afraid! Stand up with us and take the pledge.

MEN: *(Again divide the lines)*
The bastards!
There's no way!
I'm with you, Mother!
We pledge!
I won't go back to work till we get what we want!
You're right, Mother!
We won't work!
Help us, Mother, what can we do about the scabs?
We don't want to go back to work till we win our demands, but, Mother, the company has brought in scabs to take our jobs. We got nothin' but a roof and black coffee, but the company will take even that.
What do we do about the scabs?

MOTHER JONES: You men go on home and mind the children. This meeting is adjourned for all but the women. Go on now. Do as I ask. I have a sure fire plan to drive the scabs away and to drive the company bosses right up the mountain and back down their own mine shafts. We'll win this strike and when we do, I'll buy drinks for every one of you boys. Go home now.

The men take the children and start to drift off. MOTHER JONES *motions the women to come closer to her.*

MOTHER JONES: I want each and every one of you to meet me back here with mops and brooms. We're going to sweep the dirty scabs right out of the mine and off the mountain. Bring

pails, some empty and some filled with water . . . bring pots
and pans and hammers and dishpans, we'll hammer and
howl . . . and—

The lights begin to dim down on this group as MOTHER JONES *is
conspiring deliciously with them.*

MOTHER JONES: Listen to Mother! YOU DON'T HAVE TO
BE AFRAID OF ANYONE!

Lights all the way out on this scene.

Spotlight up on MOLLIE *at telephone. She is surrounded by plants
and packages, and a couple of tethered animals if possible, others in
cages perhaps. It's as if she's calling from the train station or some
shipping place home to* GUS *at their Winter quarters.*

When GUS *picks up phone, a baby spot on him. We see he's ill and
not as strong as he once was.*

*The song is a duet, sometimes they take turns—sometimes sing different
things at the same time and come in together on the chorus.*

*Lines marked with * are sung, all others spoken.*

MOLLIE: *Mr. Bailey, I miss you so.
      *Are you eatin' well?
      I'm mailin' you a corn and sausage pie
      It'll keep till the full moon.
      You try to eat it all
      And get strong enough to tell the children
      You'll be joinin' us soon
      *Oh Mr. Bailey, I miss you so.

GUS: *Yes, Mrs. Bailey, I'm keepin' warm
      *And Minnie is a perfect nurse.
      *She can manage a house
      *Keeps a tight purse
      And her husband A.W. is fine
      And we're all as happy as we could be without you.
      But you'll be joinin' us soon.

*Mrs. Bailey, I miss you so.

Mrs. Bailey?
Can Eugene lead the band?
I miss all the people,
*All the really good people
Are the crowds holding up
Are the canaries well,
They used to get sicker faster
Than this old man.

MOLLIE: *Business has not been bad, my darlin'
I was able to make a good deal on ten more wagons.
*Yes, darling, we need them
'cause we were able to trap and train
A coyote, some deer, a dancing bear
And the mostly queenly leopard cat
ever begat by nature.

GUS: *I built you a new dancin' floor
*With mirrors on the walls
*On all the doors.
*I'll even be able to see your beautiful face
*In the hardwood floors.
This winter we'll teach dancing together
Have flocks of youngin's around.

I'll see you soon and tell you
with my own eyes and arms

MOLLIE: *Oh Mr. Bailey, I do miss you so.

GUS: And you'll know you're the only
woman ever was able to start
up my old heart.

MOLLIE: I'm sending you the leaves of the perriwinkle
Grandma called it Myrtle . . .

GUS: *Mrs. Bailey, we're not really apart . . .

MOLLIE: A little wild flower from deep in the woods

It'll wake up your mind and make your blood start
*And soon you'll have your fiddle singing . . .

GUS: We've been joined forever in God's eyes.

MOLLIE: And some healing plants I picked
    'specially for you, along the trail
    *Oh Mr. Bailey, do you miss me as much as I miss you?

GUS: *Look up at your stars, our union is eternal as the sky.

MOLLIE: *Mr. Bailey, I miss you so.
    *Are you eatin' well
    I'm mailin' you a corn and sausage pie
    It'll keep till the full moon
    Ya eat it all
    And get strong enough to tell the children
    *You'll be joining us soon
    *Oh Mr. Bailey, I miss you so.

Cut to MOTHER JONES.

Enter the Women's Army on the March singing. Dawn. Leading are
MOTHER JONES *and a woman dressed in a red petticoat over a thick
cotton nightgown, wearing one black stocking and a white one. The
woman has a little red fringed shawl tied over her wild red hair. Her
face is red and her eyes are mad. The women are singing and beating
on their pots and pans. There are flags. "Marching Song for Mother
Jones and the Women's Army":*
    My body and breath were given to me
    By God, you clod
    Not by you, you screw!
    He made me King of My Being
(People may sing "She" and "Queen" if they wish)
    And He is King of my soul!

    You mole,
    He gave me whole
    Into the Universe
    You perverse boss-tyrants
    You bleedy-greedy haunts

We'll never do what you want!
God created coal
Not you—you mole!
For He made me King of my Being
And He is King of my soul!

I breathe my body
and God breathes me
I'm His personal hobby
He's set me free
For He made me King of my Being
And He is King of my soul
We work God's coal
And we want to work it whole!

I piss my piss
I sweat my sweat
And God comes to me in every kiss I kiss
And for this
I work hard for God's Bliss
For He made me King of my Being
and He is King of my soul
He made me, me—
and—He made me Free!
I am King of my Being
He is King of my Soul!

Children beat on pans and pan lids. The women are yelling, "Get
the scabs. Get the dirty scabs. Clean them out. Get the scabs.
Get the dirty scabs." *They are howling and hollering. The sheriff
comes up followed by a mule cart of coal.*

SHERIFF: *(To* MOTHER JONES*)* My dear lady. Don't frighten the
mules.

WOMAN WITH RED HAIR: *(Hits* SHERIFF *with tin pan)* To hell
with you and the mules!

The SHERIFF *falls down into the creek. The other women charge the
mules and the scab drivers. The mules snort and buck and kick. The*

scabs start to run, but are tripped and beaten by the women with mops and brooms. They dump water on them.

ALL THE WOMEN: Give 'em hell. Give 'em hell. You bet your boots we're givin' 'em hell!

MOTHER JONES: Mop up the scabs. Mop 'em up. We'll take turns keeping watch—all night and all day and all night—so's no scabs come back to take your jobs!

BLACKOUT

Cut back to MOLLIE *and* GUS *talking on phones.*

GUS: Yep, it's true
    We're gonna be grandparents . . .
    I love you too.

MOLLIE: Since you can't see us till winter
    We're sending you some friends we've found
    I'm with the shipping agent
    So you can expect by mail
    Two groundsquirrels, a very
    smart nanny goat, a piglet
    with *black* spots, a *red*
     coat and a *curly* tail,
    *and blackberry jam, and baby palms
    *a cactus, and a raccoon and
    *a *ring* tail.

GUS: *Minnie's so happy, and in great shape too . . .
    *And Mrs. Bailey . . .

MOLLIE: Mr. Bailey . . .

GUS: You'll be joining us soon?

MOLLIE: *I miss you so.

GUS: *I miss you so.

BOTH: *I miss you so.

MOLLIE: *We send our dearest love, Gus
    *We miss you more than tongues can tell.
    *And we want to see what you think of THIS surprise!
    *We've made a new version of our favorite song.
    *If you like it darlin' sing along with us please.

Segue into "Diamonds from the Stars." She motions children to come to phone.
MINNIE and GUS join in on song from other end of the phone.
MINNIE very pregnant.

GUS turns to MINNIE.

GUS: Hold the phone? Come here, Minnie, and help me hold the phone, m' arms given way.

Lights dim as "Diamonds from the Stars" ends. All freeze in a tableau with MOLLIE and the children.

Lights slowly go all the way out on GUS as he dies in the arms of MINNIE.

Music underscore.

Lights then come back to full on MOLLIE and children saying "Happy Birthday, Mollie, Happy Birthday, Grandma, Happy Birthday Aunt Mollie," etc..

As each actors says a line, she/he does something to help transform MOLLIE into an older woman., i.e., seat her in a chair, place a shawl about her, put a hat or wig on her. When the transformation is complete the actors and band members recite this toast:

Music out.

ALL: Circuses may come
    Circuses may go
    But there'll never be another
    Like you and your show.

    Long may you live
    And when you are gone

May your memory forever
Live on and on.

MOLLIE's *birthday song follows: "Mollie Bailey's 75th Birthday"*

MOLLIE: *(Singing)* Yes, I'm Mollie Bailey
I admit it, herself, the very same.
I'm Mollie Bailey
Of the Clan Bailey fame.
A Scorpio with Cancer rising
A mother reflective
A spiritual detective
And I make this claim:

Anyone can live to seventy-five!
I know some people of twenty
More dead than alive!
Go on—go on and open
Open that door you've never opened before!
I'll be back again
it's been too good to let it end.
(Reprise last seven lines with MOTHER JONES)

ALL: *(Reprise "Diamonds from the Stars."*

CURTAIN

BATTERY

BY DANIEL THERRIAULT

lectricity is the central metaphor and an expressive image for this unusual love
ory set in an electrical workshop. This young playwright has been compared
Sam Shepard and David Mamet for his superb use of language.

An English style thriller with a fascinating plot that takes intricate twists and
turns, as a husband and wife try to kill each other off, aided by a mysterious
Merchant of Death.

ESCOFFIER
KING OF CHEFS
by
Owen S. Rackleff

Tom V.H

In this one-man show set in a Monte Carlo villa at the end of the last century, the grand master of the kitchen, Escoffier, ponders a glorious return from retirement. In doing so, he relates anecdotes about the famous and shares his mouth-watering recipes with the audience.

LOOKING-GLASS

by Michael Sutton and Cynthia Mandelberg

This provocative chronicle, interspersed with fantasy sequences from ALICE I
WONDERLAND, traces the career of Charles Dodgson (better known as Lew
Carroll) from his first work on the immortal classic, to his near downfall whe
accused of immorality.

One Acts
~ And ~
Monologues
~ For ~

Women

BY ~ LUDMILLA BOLLOW

hese three haunting plays mark the arrival of a new voice in the American
heater.

SOME RAIN

by James Edward Luczak

Set in rural Alabama in 1968, the play is a bittersweet tale of a middle-age waitress whose ability to love and be loved is re-kindled by her chance encounter with a young drifter. First presented in 1982 at the Eugene O'Neill Playwright Conference and Off-Broadway on Theater Row.

SUMMIT CONFERENCE

ROBERT DAVID MacDONALD

n the Berlin chancellery in 1941, this play is a fictional encounter between
Braun and Clara Petacci. This show had a successful run on London's West
in 1982 with Glenda Jackson.

This delightful small-scale musical is about the life of Gilbert and Sullivan. It is
interspersed with some of the best known songs from the Savoy operas, including
THE PIRATES OF PENZANCE, HMS PINAFORE and THE MIKADO. This
show had a very successful run on the West End of London in 1975.